# The Poetic Principle by Edgar Allan Poe

Edgar Allan Poe (born Edgar Poe) was born in Boston Massachusetts on January 19th 1809 and was orphaned at an early age. Taken in by the Allan family his education was cut short by lack of money and he went to the military academy, West Point where he failed to become an officer.

His early literary works were poetic but he quickly turned to prose. He worked for several magazines and journals until in January 1845 The Raven was published and became an instant classic.

Thereafter followed the works for which he is now so rightly famed as a master of the mysterious and macabre. In this volume we bring you his essay on poetry, less well known than his stories, but fascinating none the less and, as an addition, helps to round out Edgar Allan Poe the Artist as well as a remarkable insight to his thoughts.

Poe died at the early age of 40 in 1849 in Baltimore, Maryland

## Index Of Contents

## The Poetic Principle

In speaking of the Poetic Principle, I have no design to be either thorough or profound. While discussing, very much at random, the essentiality of what we call Poetry, my principal purpose will be to cite for consideration, some few of those minor English or American poems which best suit my own taste, or which, upon my own fancy, have left the most definite impression. By "minor poems" I mean, of course, poems of little length. And here, in the beginning, permit me to say a few words in regard to a somewhat peculiar principle, which, whether rightfully or wrongfully, has always had its influence in my own critical estimate of the poem. I hold that a long poem does not exist. I maintain that the phrase, "a long poem," is simply a flat contradiction in terms.

I need scarcely observe that a poem deserves its title only inasmuch as it excites, by elevating the soul. The value of the poem is in the ratio of this elevating excitement. But all excitements are, through a psychal necessity, transient. That degree of excitement which would entitle a poem to be so called at all, cannot be sustained throughout a composition of any great length. After the lapse of half an hour, at the very utmost, it flags, fails, a revulsion ensues, and then the poem is, in effect, and in fact, no longer such.

There are, no doubt, many who have found difficulty in reconciling the critical dictum that the "Paradise Lost" is to be devoutly admired throughout, with the absolute impossibility of maintaining for it, during perusal, the amount of enthusiasm which that critical dictum would demand. This great work, in fact, is to be regarded as poetical, only when, losing sight of that vital requisite in all works of Art, Unity, we view it merely as a series of minor poems. If, to preserve its Unity, its totality of effect or impression, we read it (as would be necessary) at a single sitting, the result is but a constant alternation of excitement and depression. After a passage of what we feel to be true poetry, there follows, inevitably, a passage of platitude which no critical prejudgment can force us to admire; but if, upon completing the work, we read it again, omitting the first book, that is to say, commencing with the second, we shall be surprised at now finding that admirable which we before condemned, that damnable which we had previously so much admired. It follows from all this that the ultimate, aggregate, or absolute effect of even the best epic under the sun, is a nullity: and this is precisely the fact.

In regard to the Iliad, we have, if not positive proof, at least very good reason for believing it intended as a series of lyrics; but, granting the epic intention, I can say only that the work is based in an imperfect sense of art. The modem epic is, of the supposititious ancient model, but an inconsiderate and blindfold imitation. But the day of these artistic anomalies is over. If, at any time, any very long poem were popular in reality, which I doubt, it is at least clear that no very long poem will ever be popular again.

That the extent of a poetical work is, ceteris paribus, the measure of its merit, seems undoubtedly, when we thus state it, a proposition sufficiently absurd, yet we are indebted for it to the Quarterly Reviews. Surely there can be nothing in mere size, abstractly considered, there can be nothing in mere bulk, so far as a volume is concerned, which has so continuously elicited admiration from these saturnine pamphlets! A mountain, to be sure, by the mere sentiment of physical magnitude which it conveys, does impress us with a sense of the sublime, but no man is impressed after this fashion by the material grandeur of even "The Columbiad." Even the Quarterlies have not instructed us to be so impressed by it. As yet, they have not insisted on our estimating Lamar" tine by the cubic foot, or Pollock by the pound but what else are we to infer from their continual plating about "sustained effort"? If, by "sustained effort," any little gentleman has accomplished an epic, 1* us frankly commend him for the effort, if this indeed be a thing commendable, but let us forbear praising the epic on the effort's account. It is to be hoped that common sense, in the time to come, will prefer deciding upon a work of Art rather by the impression it makes, by the effect it produces, than by the time it took to impress the effect, or by the amount of "sustained effort" which had been found necessary in effecting the impression. The fact is, that perseverance is one thing and genius quite another, nor can all the Quarterlies in Christendom confound them. By and by, this proposition, with many which I have been just urging, will be received as self-evident. In the meantime, by being generally condemned as falsities, they will not be essentially damaged as truths.

On the other hand, it is clear that a poem may be improperly brief. Undue brevity degenerates into mere epigrammatism. A very short poem, while now and then producing a brilliant or vivid, never produces a profound or enduring effect. There must be the steady pressing down of the stamp upon the wax. De Beranger has wrought innumerable things, pungent and spirit-stirring, but in general they have been too imponderous to stamp themselves deeply into the public attention, and thus, as so many feathers of fancy, have been blown aloft only to be whistled down the wind.

A remarkable instance of the effect of undue brevity in depressing a poem, in keeping it out of the popular view, is afforded by the following exquisite little Serenade

I arise from dreams of thee
In the first sweet sleep of night,
When the winds are breathing low,
And the stars are shining bright.
I arise from dreams of thee,
And a spirit in my feet
Has led me, who knows how?
To thy chamber-window, sweet!

The wandering airs they faint
On the dark the silent stream
The champak odors fail
Like sweet thoughts in a dream;
The nightingale's complaint,
It dies upon her heart,
As I must die on shine,
O, beloved as thou art!

O, lift me from the grass!
I die, I faint, I fail!
Let thy love in kisses rain
On my lips and eyelids pale.
My cheek is cold and white, alas!
My heart beats loud and fast:
O, press it close to shine again,
Where it will break at last.

Very few perhaps are familiar with these lines, yet no less a poet than Shelley is their author. Their warm, yet delicate and ethereal imagination will be appreciated by all, but by none so thoroughly as by him who has himself arisen from sweet dreams of one beloved to bathe in the aromatic air of a southern midsummer night.

One of the finest poems by Willis, the very best in my opinion which he has ever written, has no doubt, through this same defect of undue brevity, been kept back from its proper position not less in the

The shadows lay along Broadway,
'Twas near the twilight-tide
And slowly there a lady fair
Was walking in her pride.
Alone walk'd she; but, viewlessly,
Walk'd spirits at her side.

Peace charm'd the street beneath her feet,
And Honor charm'd the air;
And all astir looked kind on her,
And called her good as fair
For all God ever gave to her
She kept with chary care.

She kept with care her beauties rare
From lovers warm and true
For heart was cold to all but gold,
And the rich came not to won,
But honor'd well her charms to sell.
If priests the selling do.

Now walking there was one more fair
A slight girl, lily-pale;
And she had unseen company
To make the spirit quail
'Twixt Want and Scorn she walk'd forlorn,
And nothing could avail.

No mercy now can clear her brow
From this world's peace to pray
For as love's wild prayer dissolved in air,
Her woman's heart gave way!
But the sin forgiven by Christ in Heaven
By man is cursed alway!

In this composition we find it difficult to recognize the Willis who has written so many mere "verses of society." The lines are not only richly ideal, but full of energy, while they breathe an earnestness, an evident sincerity of sentiment, for which we look in vain throughout all the other works of this author.

While the epic mania, while the idea that to merit in poetry prolixity is indispensable, has for some years past been gradually dying out of the public mind, by mere dint of its own absurdity, we find it succeeded by a heresy too palpably false to be long tolerated, but one which, in the brief period it has already endured, may be said to have accomplished more in the corruption of our Poetical Literature than all its other enemies combined. I allude to the heresy of The Didactic. It has been assumed, tacitly and avowedly, directly and indirectly, that the ultimate object of all Poetry is Truth. Every poem, it is said, should inculcate a morals and by this moral is the poetical merit of the work to be adjudged. We Americans especially have patronized this happy idea, and we Bostonians very especially have developed it in full. We have taken it into our heads that to write a poem simply for the poem's sake, and to acknowledge such to have been our design, would be to confess ourselves radically wanting in the true poetic dignity and force: but the simple fact is that would we but permit ourselves to look into our own souls we should immediately there discover that under the sun there neither exists nor can exist any work more thoroughly dignified, more supremely noble, than this very poem, this poem per se, this poem which is a poem and nothing more, this poem written solely for the poem's sake.

With as deep a reverence for the True as ever inspired the bosom of man, I would nevertheless limit, in some measure, its modes of inculcation. I would limit to enforce them. I would not enfeeble them by dissipation. The demands of Truth are severe. She has no sympathy with the myrtles. All that which is so indispensable in Song is precisely all that with which she has nothing whatever to do. It is but making her a flaunting paradox to wreathe her in gems and flowers. In enforcing a truth we need severity rather than efflorescence of language. We must be simple, precise, terse. We must be cool, calm, unimpassioned. In a word, we must be in that mood which, as nearly as possible, is the exact converse of the poetical. He must be blind indeed who does not perceive the radical and chasmal difference between the truthful and the poetical modes of inculcation. He must be theory-mad beyond redemption who, in spite of these differences, shall still persist in attempting to reconcile the obstinate oils and waters of Poetry and Truth.

Dividing the world of mind into its three most immediately obvious distinctions, we have the Pure Intellect, Taste, and the Moral Sense. I place Taste in the middle, because it is just this position which in the mind it occupies. It holds intimate relations with either extreme; but from the Moral Sense is separated by so faint a difference that Aristotle has not hesitated to place some of its operations among the virtues themselves. Nevertheless we find the offices of the trio marked with a sufficient distinction. Just as the Intellect concerns itself with Truth, so Taste informs us of the Beautiful, while the Moral Sense is regardful of Duty. Of this latter, while Conscience teaches the obligation, and Reason the expediency, Taste contents herself with displaying the charms: waging war upon Vice solely on the ground of her deformity, her disproportion, her animosity to the fitting, to the appropriate, to the harmonious, in a word, to Beauty.

An immortal instinct deep within the spirit of man is thus plainly a sense of the Beautiful. This it is which administers to his delight in the manifold forms, and sounds, and odors and sentiments amid which he exists. And just as the lily is repeated in the lake, or the eyes of Amaryllis in the mirror, so is the mere oral or written repetition of these forms, and sounds, and colors, and odors, and sentiments a duplicate source of de" light. But this mere repetition is not poetry. He who shall simply sing, with however glowing enthusiasm, or with however vivid a truth of description, of the sights, and sounds, and odors, and colors, and sentiments which greet him in common with all mankind, he, I say, has yet failed to prove his divine title. There is still a something in the distance which he has been unable to attain. We have still a thirst unquenchable, to allay which he has not shown us the crystal springs. This thirst belongs to the immortality of Man. It is at once a consequence and an indication of his perennial existence. It is the desire of the moth for the star. It is no mere appreciation of the Beauty before us, but a wild effort to reach the Beauty above. Inspired by an ecstatic prescience of the glories beyond the grave, we struggle by multiform combinations among the things and thoughts of Time to attain a portion of that Loveliness whose very elements perhaps appertain to eternity alone. And thus when by Poetry, or when by Music, the most entrancing of the poetic moods, we find ourselves melted into tears, we weep then, not as the Abbate Gravina supposes, through excess of pleasure, but through a certain petulant, impatient sorrow at our inability to grasp now, wholly, here on earth, at once and for ever, those divine and rapturous joys of which through' the poem, or through the music, we attain to but brief and indeterminate glimpses.

The struggle to apprehend the supernal Loveliness, this struggle, on the part of souls fittingly constituted, has given to the world all that which it (the world) has ever been enabled at once to understand and to feel as poetic.

The Poetic Sentiment, of course, may develop itself in various modes, in Painting, in Sculpture, in Architecture, in the Dance, very especially in Music, and very peculiarly, and with a wide field, in the com position of the Landscape Garden. Our present theme, however, has regard only to its manifestation in words. And here let me speak briefly on the topic of rhythm. Contenting myself with the certainty that Music, in its various modes of metre, rhythm, and rhyme, is of so vast a moment in Poetry as never to be wisely rejected is so vitally important an adjunct, that he is simply silly who declines its assistance, I will not now pause to maintain its absolute essentiality. It is in Music perhaps that the soul most nearly attains the great end for which, when inspired by the Poetic Sentiment, it struggles: the creation of supernal Beauty. It may be, indeed, that here this sublime end is, now and then, attained in fact. We are often made to feel, with a shivering delight, that from an earthly harp are stricken notes which cannot have been unfamiliar to the angels. And thus there can be little doubt that in the union of Poetry with Music in its popular sense, we shall find the widest field for the Poetic development. The old Bards and Minnesingers had advantages which we do not possess and Thomas Moore, singing his own songs, was, in the most legitimate manner, perfecting them as poems.

To recapitulate then: I would define, in brief, the Poetry of words as The Rhythmical Creation of Beauty. Its sole arbiter is Taste. With the Intellect or with the Conscience it has only collateral relations. Unless incidentally, it has no concern whatever either with Duty or with Truth.

A few words, however, in explanation. That pleasure which is at once the most pure, the most elevating, and the most intense, is derived, I maintain, from the contemplation of the Beautiful. In the contemplation of Beauty we alone find it possible to attain that pleasurable elevation, or excitement of the soul, which we recognize as the Poetic Sentiment, and which is so easily distinguished from Truth, which is the satisfaction of the Reason, or from Passion, which is the excitement of the heart. I make Beauty, therefore, using the word as inclusive of the sublime, I make Beauty the province of the poem, simply because it is an obvious rule of Art that effects should be made to spring as directly as possible from their causes: no one as yet having been weak enough to deny that the peculiar elevation in question is at least most readily attainable in the poem. It by no means follows, however, that the incitements of Passion' or the precepts of Duty, or even the lessons of Truth, may not be introduced into a poem, and with advantage; for they may subserve incidentally, in various ways, the general purposes of the work: but the true artist will always contrive to tone them down in proper subjection to that Beauty which is the atmosphere and the real essence of the poem.

I cannot better introduce the few poems which I shall present for your consideration, than by the citation of the Proem to Longfellow's "Waif":

The day is done, and the darkness
Falls from the wings of Night,
As a feather is wafted downward
From an Eagle in his flight.

I see the lights of the village
Gleam through the rain and the mist,
And a feeling of sadness comes o'er me,
That my soul cannot resist;

A feeling of sadness and longing,
That is not akin to pain,
And resembles sorrow only
As the mist resembles the rain.

Come, read to me some poem,
Some simple and heartfelt lay,
That shall soothe this restless feeling,
And banish the thoughts of day.

Not from the grand old masters,
Not from the bards sublime,
Whose distant footsteps echo
Through the corridors of Time.

For, like strains of martial music,
Their mighty thoughts suggest
Life's endless toil and endeavor;
And to-night I long for rest.

Read from some humbler poet,
Whose songs gushed from his heart,
As showers from the clouds of summer,
Or tears from the eyelids start;

Who through long days of labor,
And nights devoid of ease,
Still heard in his soul the music
Of wonderful melodies.

Such songs have power to quiet
The restless pulse of care,
And come like the benediction
That follows after prayer.

Then read from the treasured volume
The poem of thy choice,
And lend to the rhyme of the poet
The beauty of thy voice.

And the night shall be filled with music,
And the cares that infest the day
Shall fold their tents like the Arabs,
And as silently steal away.

With no great range of imagination, these lines have been justly admired for their delicacy of expression. Some of the images are very effective. Nothing can be better than

the bards sublime,
Whose distant footsteps echo
Down the corridors of Time.

The idea of the last quatrain is also very effective. The poem on the whole, however, is chiefly to be admired for the graceful insouciance of its metre, so well in accordance with the character of the sentiments, and especially for the ease of the general manner. This "ease" or naturalness, in a literary style, it has long been the fashion to regard as ease in appearance alone as a point of really difficult attainment. But not so: a natural manner is difficult only to him who should never meddle with it, to the unnatural. It is but the result of writing with the understanding, or with the instinct, that the tone, in composition, should always be that which the mass of mankind would adopt and must perpetually vary, of course, with the occasion. The author who, after the fashion of "The North American Review," should be upon all occasions merely "quiet," must necessarily upon many occasions be simply silly, or stupid; and has no more right to be considered "easy" or "natural" than a Cockney exquisite, or than the sleeping Beauty in the waxworks.

Among the minor poems of Bryant, none has so much impressed me as the one which he entitles "June." I quote only a portion of it:

There, through the long, long summer hours,
The golden light should lie,
And thick young herbs and groups of flowers
Stand in their beauty by.
The oriole should build and tell
His love-tale, close beside my cell;
The idle butterfly
Should rest him there, and there be heard
The housewife-bee and humming bird.

And what, if cheerful shouts at noon,
Come, from the village sent,
Or songs of maids, beneath the moon,
With fairy laughter blent?
And what if, in the evening light,
Betrothed lovers walk in sight
Of my low monument?
I would the lovely scene around
Might know no sadder sight nor sound.

I know, I know I should not see
The season's glorious show,
Nor would its brightness shine for me;
Nor its wild music flow;
But if, around my place of sleep,
The friends I love should come to weep,
They might not haste to go.
Soft airs and song, and the light and bloom,
Should keep them lingering by my tomb.

These to their soften'd hearts should bear
The thoughts of what has been,
And speak of one who cannot share
The gladness of the scene;
Whose part in all the pomp that fills

The circuit of the summer hills,
Is that his grave is green;
And deeply would their hearts rejoice
To hear again his living voice.

The rhythmical flow here is even voluptuous, nothing could be more melodious. The poem has always affected me in a remarkable manner. The intense melancholy which seems to well up, perforce, to the surface of all the poet's cheerful sayings about his grave, we find thrilling us to the soul, while there is the truest poetic elevation in the thrill. The impression left is one of a pleasurable sadness. And if, in the remaining compositions which I shall introduce to you, there be more or less of a similar tone always apparent, let me remind you that (how or why we know not) this certain taint of sadness is inseparably connected with all the higher manifestations of true Beauty. It is, nevertheless,

A feeling of sadness and longing
That is not akin to pain,
And resembles sorrow only
As the mist resembles the rain.

The taint of which I speak is clearly perceptible even in a poem so full of brilliancy and spirit as "The Health" of Edward Coate Pinckney:

I fill this cup to one made up
Of loveliness alone,
A woman, of her gentle sex
The seeming paragon;
To whom the better elements
And kindly stars have given
A form so fair that, like the air,
'Tis less of earth than heaven.

Her every tone is music's own,
Like those of morning birds,
And something more than melody
Dwells ever in her words;
The coinage of her heart are they,
And from her lips each flows
As one may see the burden'd bee
Forth issue from the rose.

Affections are as thoughts to her,
The measures of her hours;
Her feelings have the flagrancy,
The freshness of young flowers;
And lovely passions, changing oft,
So fill her, she appears
The image of themselves by turns,
The idol of past years!

Of her bright face one glance will trace
A picture on the brain,
And of her voice in echoing hearts
A sound must long remain;
But memory, such as mine of her,
So very much endears,
When death is nigh my latest sigh
Will not be life's, but hers.

I fill'd this cup to one made up
Of loveliness alone,
A woman, of her gentle sex
The seeming paragon
Her health! and would on earth there stood,
Some more of such a frame,
That life might be all poetry,
And weariness a name.

It was the misfortune of Mr. Pinckney to have been born too far south. Had he been a New Englander, it is probable that he would have been ranked as the first of American lyrists by that magnanimous cabal which has so long controlled the destinies of American Letters, in conducting the thing called "The North American Review." The poem just cited is especially beautiful; but the poetic elevation which it induces we must refer chiefly to our sympathy in the poet's enthusiasm. We pardon his hyperboles for the evident earnestness with which they are uttered.

It was by no means my design, however, to expatiate upon the merits of what I should read you. These will necessarily speak for themselves. Boccalini, in his "Advertisements from Parnassus," tells us that Zoilus once presented Apollo a very caustic criticism upon a very admirable book: whereupon the god asked him for the beauties of the work. He replied that he only busied himself about the errors. On hearing this, Apollo, handing him a sack of unwinnowed wheat, bade him pick out all the chaff for his reward.

Now this fable answers very well as a hit at the critics but I am by no means sure that the god was in the right. I am by no means certain that the true limits of the critical duty are not grossly misunderstood. Excellence, in a poem especially, may be considered in the light of an axiom, which need only be properly put, to become self-evident. It is not excellence if it require to be demonstrated as such: and thus to point out too particularly the merits of a work of Art, is to admit that they are not merits altogether.

Among the "Melodies" of Thomas Moore is one whose distinguished character as a poem proper seems to have been singularly left out of view. I allude to his lines beginning "Come, rest in this bosom." The intense energy of their expression is not surpassed by anything in Byron. There are two of the lines in which a sentiment is conveyed that embodies the all in all of the divine passion of Love, a sentiment which, perhaps, has found its echo in more, and in more passionate, human hearts than any other single sentiment ever embodied in words:

Come, rest in this bosom, my own stricken deer
Though the herd have fled from thee, thy home is still here;

Here still is the smile, that no cloud can o'ercast,
And a heart and a hand all thy own to the last.

Oh! what was love made for, if 'tis not the same
Through joy and through torment, through glory and shame?
I know not, I ask not, if guilt's in that heart,
I but know that I love thee, whatever thou art.

Thou hast call'd me thy Angel in moments of bliss,
And thy Angel I'll be, 'mid the horrors of this,
Through the furnace, unshrinking, thy steps to pursue,
And shield thee, and save thee, or perish there too!

It has been the fashion of late days to deny Moore Imagination, while granting him Fancy, a distinction originating with Coleridge, than whom no man more fully comprehended the great powers of Moore. The fact is, that the fancy of this poet so far predominates over all his other faculties, and over the fancy of all other men, as to have induced, very naturally, the idea that he is fanciful only. But never was there a greater mistake. Never was a grosser wrong done the fame of a true poet. In the compass of the English language I can call to mind no poem more profoundry, more weirdly imaginative, in the best sense, than the lines commencing "I would I were by that dim lake" which are the com. position of Thomas Moore. I regret that I am unable to remember them.

One of the noblest, and, speaking of Fancy, one of the most singularly fanciful of modern poets, was Thomas Hood. His "Fair Ines" had always for me an inexpressible charm:

O saw ye not fair Ines?
She's gone into the West,
To dazzle when the sun is down,
And rob the world of rest;
She took our daylight with her,
The smiles that we love best,
With morning blushes on her cheek,
And pearls upon her breast.

O turn again, fair Ines,
Before the fall of night,
For fear the moon should shine alone,
And stars unrivalltd bright;
And blessed will the lover be
That walks beneath their light,
And breathes the love against thy cheek
I dare not even write!

Would I had been, fair Ines,
That gallant cavalier,
Who rode so gaily by thy side,
And whisper'd thee so near!
Were there no bonny dames at home

Or no true lovers here,
That he should cross the seas to win
The dearest of the dear?

I saw thee, lovely Ines,
Descend along the shore,
With bands of noble gentlemen,
And banners waved before;
And gentle youth and maidens gay,
And snowy plumes they wore;
It would have been a beauteous dream,
If it had been no more!

Alas, alas, fair Ines,
She went away with song,
With music waiting on her steps,
And shootings of the throng;
But some were sad and felt no mirth,
But only Music's wrong,
In sounds that sang Farewell, Farewell,
To her you've loved so long.

Farewell, farewell, fair Ines,
That vessel never bore
So fair a lady on its deck,
Nor danced so light before,
Alas for pleasure on the sea,
And sorrow on the shorel
The smile that blest one lover's heart
Has broken many more!

"The Haunted House," by the same author, is one of the truest poems ever written, one of the truest, one of the most unexceptionable, one of the most thoroughly artistic, both in its theme and in its execution. It is, moreover, powerfully ideal, imaginative. I regret that its length renders it unsuitable for the purposes of this lecture. In place of it permit me to offer the universally appreciated "Bridge of Sighs":

One more Unfortunate,
Weary of breath,
Rashly importunate
Gone to her death!

Take her up tenderly,
Lift her with care;
Fashion'd so slenderly,
Young and so fair!

Look at her garments
Clinging like cerements;

Whilst the wave constantly
Drips from her clothing;
Take her up instantly,
Loving not loathing.

Touch her not scornfully;
Think of her mournfully,
Gently and humanly;
Not of the stains of her,
All that remains of her
Now is pure womanly.

Make no deep scrutiny
Into her mutiny
Rash and undutiful;
Past all dishonor,
Death has left on her
Only the beautiful.

Where the lamps quiver
So far in the river,
With many a light
From window and casement
From garret to basement,
She stood, with amazement,
Houseless by night.

The bleak wind of March
Made her tremble and shiver,
But not the dark arch,
Or the black flowing river:
Mad from life's history,
Glad to death's mystery,
Swift to be hurl'd
Anywhere, anywhere
Out of the world!

In she plunged boldly,
No matter how coldly
The rough river ran,
Over the brink of it,
Picture it, think of it,
Dissolute Man!
Lave in it, drink of it
Then, if you can!

Still, for all slips of hers,
One of Eve's family
Wipe those poor lips of hers

Oozing so clammily,
Loop up her tresses
Escaped from the comb,
Her fair auburn tresses;
Whilst wonderment guesses
Where was her home?

Who was her father?
Who was her mother?
Had she a sister?
Had she a brother?
Or was there a dearer one
Still, and a nearer one
Yet, than all other?

Alas! for the rarity
Of Christian charity
Under the sun!
Oh! it was pitiful!
Near a whole city full,
Home she had none.

Sisterly, brotherly,
Fatherly, motherly,
Feelings had changed:
Love, by harsh evidence,
Thrown from its eminence;
Even God's providence
Seeming estranged.

Take her up tenderly;
Lift her with care;
Fashion'd so slenderly,
Young, and so fair!
Ere her limbs frigidly
Stiffen too rigidly,
Decently, kindly,
Smooth and compose them;
And her eyes, close them,
Staring so blindly!

Dreadfully staring
Through muddy impurity,
As when with the daring
Last look of despairing
Fixed on futurity.

Perhishing gloomily,
Spurred by contumely,

Cold inhumanity,
Burning insanity,
Into her rest,
Cross her hands humbly,
As if praying dumbly,
Over her breast!
Owning her weakness,
Her evil behavior,
And leaving, with meekness,
Her sins to her Saviour!

The vigor of this poem is no less remarkable than its pathos. The versification although carrying the fanciful to the very verge of the fantastic, is nevertheless admirably adapted to the wild insanity which is the thesis of the poem.

Among the minor poems of Lord Byron is one which has never received from the critics the praise which it undoubtedly deserves:

Though the day of my destiny's over,
And the star of my fate bath declined
Thy soft heart refused to discover
The faults which so many could find;
Though thy soul with my grief was acquainted,
It shrunk not to share it with me,
And the love which my spirit bath painted
It never bath found but in thee.

Then when nature around me is smiling,
The last smile which answers to mine,
I do not believe it beguiling,
Because it reminds me of shine;
And when winds are at war with the ocean,
As the breasts I believed in with me,
If their billows excite an emotion,
It is that they bear me from thee.

Though the rock of my last hope is shivered,
And its fragments are sunk in the wave,
Though I feel that my soul is delivered
To pain, it shall not be its slave.
There is many a pang to pursue me:
They may crush, but they shall not contemn
They may torture, but shall not subdue me
'Tis of thee that I think, not of them.

Though human, thou didst not deceive me,
Though woman, thou didst not forsake,
Though loved, thou forborest to grieve me,
Though slandered, thou never couldst shake,

Though trusted, thou didst not disclaim me,
Though parted, it was not to fly,
Though watchful, 'twas not to defame me,
Nor mute, that the world might belie.

Yet I blame not the world, nor despise it,
Nor the war of the many with one
If my soul was not fitted to prize it,
'Twas folly not sooner to shun:
And if dearly that error bath cost me,
And more than I once could foresee,
I have found that whatever it lost me,
It could not deprive me of thee.

From the wreck of the past, which bath perished,
Thus much I at least may recall,
It bath taught me that which I most cherished
Deserved to be dearest of all:
In the desert a fountain is springing,
In the wide waste there still is a tree,
And a bird in the solitude singing,
Which speaks to my spirit of thee.

Although the rhythm here is one of the most difficult, the versification could scarcely be improved. No nobler theme ever engaged the pen of poet. It is the soul-elevating idea that no man can consider himself entitled to complain of Fate while in his adversity he still retains the unwavering love of woman.

From Alfred Tennyson, although in perfect sincerity I regard him as the noblest poet that ever lived, I have left myself time to cite only a very brief specimen. I call him, and think him the noblest of poets, not because the impressions he produces are at all times the most profound, not because the poetical excitement which he induces is at all times the most intense but because it is at all times the most ethereal, in other words, the most elevating and most pure. No poet is so little of the earth, earthy. What I am about to read is from his last long poem, "The Princess":

Tears, idle tears, I know not what they mean,
Tears from the depth of some divine despair
Rise in the heart, and gather to the eyes,
In looking on the happy Autumn fields,
And thinking of the days that are no more.

Fresh as the first beam glittering on a sail,
That brings our friends up from the underworld,
Sad as the last which reddens over one
That sinks with all we love below the verge;
So sad, so fresh, the days that are no more.

Ah, sad and strange as in dark summer dawns
The earliest pipe of half-awaken'd birds
To dying ears, when unto dying eyes
The casement slowly grows a glimmering square;
So sad, so strange, the days that are no more.

Dear as remember'd kisses after death,
And sweet as those by hopeless fancy feign'd
On lips that are for others; deep as love,
Deep as first love, and wild with all regret;
O Death in Life, the days that are no more.

Thus, although in a very cursory and imperfect manner, I have endeavored to convey to you my conception of the Poetic Principle. It has been my purpose to suggest that, while this principle itself is strictly and simply the Human Aspiration for Supernal Beauty, the manifestation of the Principle is always found in an elevating excitement of the soul, quite independent of that passion which is the intoxication of the Heart, or of that truth which is the satisfaction of the Reason. For in regard to passion, alas! its tendency is to degrade rather than to elevate the Soul. Love, on the contrary, Love, the true, the divine Eros, the Uranian as distinguished from the Diona~an Venus is unquestionably the purest and truest of all poetical themes. And in regard to Truth, if, to be sure, through the attainment of a truth we are led to perceive a harmony where none was apparent before, we experience at once the true poetical effect; but this effect is referable to the harmony alone, and not in the least degree to the truth which merely served to render the harmony manifest.

We shall reach, however, more immediately a distinct conception of what the true Poetry is, by mere reference to a few of the simple elements which induce in the Poet himself the poetical effect He recognizes the ambrosia which nourishes his soul in the bright orbs that shine in Heaven, in the volutes of the flower, in the clustering of low shrubberies, in the waving of the grain-fields, in the slanting of tall eastern trees, in the blue distance of mountains, in the grouping of clouds, in the twinkling of half-hidden brooks, in the gleaming of silver rivers, in the repose of sequestered lakes, in the star-mirroring depths of lonely wells. He perceives it in the songs of birds, in the harp of Bolos, in the sighing of the night-wind, in the repining voice of the forest, in the surf that complains to the shore, in the fresh breath of the woods, in the scent of the violet, in the voluptuous perfume of the hyacinth, in the suggestive odour that comes to him at eventide from far distant undiscovered islands, over dim oceans, illimitable and unexplored. He owns it in all noble thoughts, in all unworldly motives, in all holy impulses, in all chivalrous, generous, and self-sacrificing deeds. He feels it in the beauty of woman, in the grace of her step, in the lustre of her eye, in the melody of her voice, in her soft laughter, in her sigh, in the harmony of the rustling of her robes. He deeply feels it in her winning endearments, in her burning enthusiasms, in her gentle charities, in her meek and devotional endurances but above all, ah, far above all, he kneels to it, he worships it in the faith, in the purity, in the strength, in the altogether divine majesty of her love.

Let me conclude by, the recitation of yet another brief poem, one very different in character from any that I have before quoted. It is by Motherwell, and is called "The Song of the Cavalier." With our modern and altogether rational ideas of the absurdity and impiety of warfare, we are not precisely in that frame of mind best adapted to sympathize with the sentiments, and thus to appreciate the real excellence of the poem. To do this fully we must identify ourselves in fancy with the soul of the old cavalier:

Then mounte! then mounte, brave gallants all,
And don your helmes amaine:
Deathe's couriers. Fame and Honor call
No shrewish teares shall fill your eye
When the sword-hilt's in our hand,
Heart-whole we'll part, and no whit sighe
For the fayrest of the land;
Let piping swaine, and craven wight,
Thus weepe and poling crye,
Our business is like men to fight.


### Edgar Allan Poe – A Short Biography

Edgar Allan Poe's career as an author, poet, editor and critic contains a number of firsts; as one of the earliest practitioners of the short story, the invention of the detective fiction genre is widely attributed to him, while he also contributed to the newly-emergent science fiction genre. Moreover, he was the first of the well-known American writers to attempt to earn a living solely through his writing, ensuring a life and career which were fraught with financial difficulty and stress. A proponent of the American Romantic Movement, much of his writing involved mystery and the macabre, and he is famed for his work in the Gothic style, a genre which was in high demand by the public and in which his attention to the question of death, decay, reanimation and mourning is considered some of the finest of the genre. While much of his attention to these recurrent themes was at the behest of the reading public to whose literary tastes he, as a professional writer, had to cater, it also stood in opposition to the popular notions of transcendentalism  with which he strongly disagreed.

He was born Edgar Poe on January 19th, 1809, in Boston, Massachusetts. Both his parents, David Poe, Jr. and Elizabeth Arnold Hopkins Poe, were actors, and he was the second of three children, between his elder brother William Henry Leonard and his younger sister Rosalie. Of Irish descent, the Poe lineage began in America after the children's grandfather, David Poe, Sr., had emigrated there from Cavan sometime around the year 1750. It is likely that Edgar was named after the namesake character in Shakespeare's King Lear, a play which the thespian couple were performing at the time of his birth. A year later, however, his father abandoned the family. Though the exact reason is unclear, it is conceivable that it was due to unfavourable comparisons between his acting talent and that of his wife, for he was widely considered inferior. Indeed, one critic said of the two, "the lady was young and pretty, and evinced talent both as a singer and actress; the gentleman was literally nothing." After having Edgar, the family's financial situation became somewhat precarious, prompting David Jr., a hot-headed, impatient alcoholic to flee, both from the family and from historical record. Eliza sustained the family for a time while pregnant with Rosalie, to whom she gave birth in 1810, though she died shortly thereafter from consumption. Poe was then taken into the care of John Allan, a successful Scottish tobacco, cloth and wheat merchant in Richmond, Virginia. Alongside this business, he made further financial gain trading in tombstones and slaves. Acting as a foster family, the Allans looked after Poe, though they never formally adopted him.

In 1812 the Allans had Poe baptised in the Episcopal Church. John would proceed to alternately spoil and discipline Poe until 1815 when the family sailed for Britain, landing briefly in Irvine, Scotland, where Allan was born, before rejoining their extended family in London in 1816. While in Irvine, Poe attended the grammar school, though on their arrival in London he boarded in Chelsea until 1817, whereupon he was sent to the Reverend John Bransby's Manor House School in Stoke Newington, a suburb which then was four miles north of London. The Allans returned, with Poe, to Richmond in 1820, where he continued his education. Notably in 1824 Poe served as the Lieutenant of the Richmond youth honour guard during the celebrated visit to Richmond of the Marquis de Lafayette, part of his tour of the 24 States of the United States of America, marking the nation's 50th anniversary and intended to instill the spirit of 1776 in a new generation of free Americans. In March 1825, John Allan's uncle and business benefactor, one of the richest men in Richmond, died, leaving Allan several acres of real estate. This inheritance was estimated at $750,000, and Allan marked the sudden and considerable expansion of his wealth by purchasing a two-storey brick home, named Moldavia.

Poe now became engaged to Sarah Elmira Royster, despite her father's disapproval and endeavours to intercept and destroy all love letters between the pair. He would later write that his disapproval was more because of their young age than his estimations of Poe himself, though he did consider him poorly suited due to his social and financial status as an orphan. Poe subsequently registered at the newly established University of Virginia in February 1826, to read ancient and modern languages. The University was, at only one year old, still very much in its infancy, and had been established on the ideals of its founder, Thomas Jefferson, though its strict rules against gambling, tobacco and alcohol, guns and horses were largely ignored. One of Jefferson's influences was the enactment of a system of self-government, whereby students chose their own studies, made their own boarding arrangements and held themselves responsible for their wrongdoings, expected to act honestly and decently towards their peers and their superiors. While here Poe lost touch with Royster, owing to her father's interference, and became estranged from Allan, owing to the gambling debts he accumulated. Claiming that Allan had not given him enough money for class registration, the purchasing of educational materials and furnishings for his dormitory, Poe's debts continued to increase, even after Allan send additional money and clothes. Meanwhile Royster, who had come to believe that Poe had forgotten her since their loss of contact, proceeded to marry Alexander B. Shelton, whose strong business connections and wealthy family rendered him favourable to Royster's father. The combination of this rejection from his sweetheart, his foster father's disapproval and the general feeling of unwelcomeness he had while in Richmond, caused him to abandon his education, travelling to Boston in April 1827, taking odd jobs as a clerk and newspaper writer to sustain himself.

However, this employment was too irregular and, on May 27th 1827, unable to support himself, Poe enlisted as a Private in the United States Army. He used the name Edgar A. Perry and claimed to be 22, though he was in fact only 18. Earning five dollars per month while serving at Ford Independence in Boston Harbour, he released his first book, a collection of poetry entitled Tamerlane and Other Poems, that same year, attributed with the byline "by a Bostonian". It printed only 50 copies and received no critical attention. Poe's regiment was then posted to Fort Moultrie in South Carolina, travelling there on November 8th 1827 by ship on the brig Waltham.

He was promoted to the position of 'artificer' as an enlisted tradesman preparing shells for the artillery, and with this promotion his monthly pay doubled. After two years in service he had achieved the rank of Sergeant Major for Artillery, the highest rank achievable by a noncommissioned officer, and he now sought to curtail his five year enlistment some three years early. Revealing his true identity and circumstances to his commanding officer, Lieutenant Howard, he would only be allowed early discharge on the condition that he reconcile with Allan. Poe subsequently wrote to Allan, though he received little sympathy; Poe wrote several times only to be met with the same position. It is thought that Allan didn't even write to Poe to inform him of the illness of his foster mother, Frances. She eventually died on February 28th, 1829, and Poe visited the day after her burial. Conceivably softened by her death, Allan relented and assented to support Poe in his endeavours to achieve discharge in order to receive appointment to the United States Military Academy at West Point.

Having secured a replacement to complete the terms of his enlistment for him, Poe was discharged on April 15th, 1829. Prior to entering West Point he moved back to Baltimore for short time to stay with his recently widowed aunt Maria Clemm, her daughter Virginia Eliza, his brother Henry and his invalid grandmother Elizabeth Cairnes Poe. During this time he published his second book, Al Aaraaf, Tamerlane and Minor Poems, in Baltimore in 1829. Matriculating as a cadet in West Point on July 1st, 1830, he was eventually disowned by the Allan family following John Allan's remarriage and the bitter quarrels which ensued over the children born to Allan out of affairs. He chose to leave West Point by getting intentionally court-martialed, tried for gross neglect of duty and disobedience of orders for refusing to attend classes, church and formations. Pleading not guilty, knowing that he would be found guilty and that this would result in dismissal, he was released from the military on February 8th, 1831. Following this he made for New York that same month, releasing a third book, simply entitled Poems, financed with the help of many of his fellow cadets at West Point, many of whom donated 75 cents towards a total amount of $170 on the expectation of verses similar in nature to those satirical lines he had been writing at the time about his commanding officers. It was printed by Elam Bliss of New York, labeled as a second edition, and included a page with the dedication "To the U.S. Corps of Cadets this volume is respectfully dedicated". it included a further reprint of the long poems 'Tamerlane' and 'Al Aaraaf' alongside six previously unpublished poems including early versions of 'To Helen', 'Israfel' and 'The City in the Sea'. Again he returned to the family in Baltimore in March 1831, though his elder brother Henry, whose ill-health due in part to alcoholism had been steadily worsening, died on August 1st 1831.

It was only after his brother's death that Poe began in earnest to develop his career as a writer, though at the time the state of American publishing would make it continuously difficult for him, with a lack of international copyright law meaning publishers often pirated copies of British work, rather than commissioning new work by Americans, while the Panic of 1837, a financial crisis and major recession which saw the collapse of banks and businesses, made publishers very cautious in their commissions and publication; indeed, although there was a boom in journals and periodicals fuelled by new technology which seemed out of context with the recession, many of these lasted but a few issues. Publishers would often either underpay their writers, pay them late or sometimes even not at all. Throughout this career, then, Poe often found himself humiliated by the need to plead for money and assistance.

The continued failure of his early attempts at poetry saw him turn his attention to prose, placing a few stories in a Philadelphian publication and in 1833 gaining recognition and receiving a prize from the Baltimore Saturday Visiter for his short story MS. Found in a Bottle. The success of this story garnered the attention of John P. Kennedy, a Baltimorean of considerable wealth, importance and influence. Kennedy helped Poe with placing his stories while introducing him to Thomas R. White, editor of the Southern Literary Messenger based in Richmond. As a result of this introduction, Poe became editor of the periodical in August 1835, though he was discharged only a few weeks later after having been caught drunk at work by White. Before this dismissal, however, he was working on what would be his only drama, Politian, though he did not complete the work. Its first half was published in 1835 in the Southern Literary Messenger under the title 'Scenes from an Unpublished Drama', and the second half was designed to follow in the same publication, though it would never materialise. Again, it received poor reviews, and, along with the failure of his earlier long poems, pointed him towards the short story form which had brought him success two years earlier. Following his removal from the periodical he returned to Baltimore and, in secret, married his cousin, Virginia. She was 13 and he was 26, though her age is listed as 21 on the marriage certificate.

Poe, having promised good behaviour to White, was subsequently reinstated at the periodical, returning to Richmond with Virginia and her mother, and he remained with the Southern Literary Messenger until January 1831. Poe claimed that, during his time there, the periodical's circulation increased from 700 to 3,500, and within these pages were published several of his poems, book reviews, works of criticism and short stories. Midway through this period of success, he had a second wedding ceremony to publicly marry Virginia, on 16th May, 1836. 1838 saw the publication of The Narrative of Arthur Gordon Pym of Nantucket, which saw wide and largely favourable reviews. In summer of the following year, he received the post of assistant editor at Burton's Gentleman's Magazine, a publication in which he placed several articles, stories and reviews, which furthered the reputation he had established for himself at the Southern Literary Herald as a vigorous critic. Alongside this editorial work, he published his collection Tales of the Grotesque and the Arabesque in two volumes, though it made little money and received mixed reviews. After almost a year Poe left Burton's and took a position as an assistant at Graham's Magazine.

In June 1840 Poe had the intention of starting his own journal, The Stylus, and he published his prospectus accordingly. Its title was initially intended to be The Penn, a pun on its location in Philadelphia, Pennsylvania. He bought advertising space for the prospectus in the June 6th, 1840 issue of the Philadelphia Saturday Evening Post, writing "Prospectus of the Penn Magazine, a Monthly Literary journal to be edited and published in the city of Philadelphia by Edgar A. Poe", though the journal was never actually produced before his death. Seeking to secure a position with the Tyler administration by pretending to be a member of the Whig party, he hoped to be appointed to the Custom House in Philadelphia with support from President Tyler's son Robert, an acquaintance of his his friend Frederick Thomas. However, he failed to show up for a meeting to discuss the appointment with Thomas in mid-September 1842, claiming to have been sick, though Thomas knew it to be more likely that he had been drunk. He was promised an appointment, though all positions were eventually filled by others.

On an evening in January 1842, Virginia began to show early signs of consumption, while she was singing and playing the piano, which Poe would later describe as breaking a blood vessel in her throat. Her recovery was only partial, and the stress of her illness led Poe to drink more and more heavily. He also left his position at Graham's in the hope of achieving a position within the government, returning to New York where he briefly worked at the Evening Mirror before he took the position of editor at the Broadway Journal, of which he would later come to be sole owner. It was here that he alienated himself from other writers by publicly accusing Henry Wadsworth Longfellow, the poet, of plagiarism, though Longfellow would never respond. 'The Raven', arguably Poe's most successful work, appeared in the Evening Mirror on January 29th 1845, quickly becoming a popular sensation. Despite it making him a household name almost instantaneously, he received a mere $9 for the work, even though it was concurrently published in The American Review: A Whig Journal under the pseudonym 'Quarles'.

The Broadway Journal collapsed in January 1846, and Poe moved to a cottage in the Fordham section of The Bronx, New York, where Virginia died on January 30th, 1847. Her death left him increasingly unstable, and Poe attempted the courtship of the poet Sarah Helen Whitman who lived in Providence, Rhode Island, which failed owing to his excessive drinking and erratic behaviour, though there is clear evidence that her mother's intervention did much to sabotage the relationship. Following this, in 1848 Poe returned to Richmond and resumed a relationship with his childhood sweetheart Sarah Elmira Royster, to whom he had been engaged and whom he had subsequently lost while at the University of Virginia to Alexander B. Shelton, but who had died in 1848. Royster remembers his arrival, writing "I was ready to go to church and a servant told me that a gentleman in the parlor wanted to see me. I went down and was amazed to see him—but knew him instantly". She had become very religious, and was very beautiful. She is remembered by a friend;

Her eyes were a deep blue, her hair brown, touched with grey, her nose thin and patrician ... Her voice was very low, soft and sweet, her manners exquisitely refined, and intellectually she was a woman of education and force of character. Her distinguishing qualities were gentleness and womanliness.

They fell in love after she attended a lecture he gave in Richmond, and though they discussed marriage they resolved not to, due in part to her children's disapproval and owing to the stipulation in Shelton's will that her $100,000 inheritance from his estate would be reduced by three-quarters.

Only a few weeks after he left Royster, he was found on 3rd October 1849, delirious, "in great distress, and ... in need of immediate assistance", as stated by Joseph W. Walker, who found him. Though he was immediately taken to Washington Medical College, he died on Sunday October 7th, 1848, at 0500. At no point between being found and his death was he sufficiently coherent to explain exactly what had happened to him, though he was wearing clothes which were not his own and is said to have repeatedly uttered the name 'Reynolds' on the night before he died; however, nobody could establish to which Reynolds he was referring. His final words were, allegedly, "Lord help my poor soul", though all records of his death, including his death certificate, have been lost. His death was reported by newspapers at the time as 'congestion of the brain' or 'cerebral inflammation', both common euphemisms for death from such disreputable causes as alcoholism, though this was speculation and the actual cause of his death remains a mystery. Various suggestions have been made, including rabies, syphilis, cholera and epilepsy, or the more sinister accusation that he was killed as a result of a particular political vote. On the day of his burial, a long obituary appeared in the New York Tribune, signed 'Ludwig', beginning "Edgar Allan Poe is dead. He died in Baltimore the day before yesterday. This announcement will startle many, but few will be grieved by it". Shortly thereafter 'Ludwig' was identified as Rufus Wilmot Griswold, a fellow editor and critic who had borne a grudge against Poe since 1842. He managed to become Poe's literary executor and sought to destroy his reputation, writing a biographical article entitled 'Memoir of the Author' in 1850, in which he made various unsupported claims about drug-use and alcoholism which, though Poe's friends vehemently refuted the article, became the popularly accepted posthumous portrait of the man. Griswold went so far as to forge letters which evidenced his smears, and Poe's readership were eager to accept this image of the man for the excitement of reading such macabre work written by someone so 'evil'. Despite Griswold's attempts, though, the genius of Poe's narrative vision and style would outlive this negative portrayal of him, and he is widely remembered as one of the American Romantic Movement's most prominent writers, and certainly one of the most significant proponents of the Gothic style.

www.ingramcontent.com/pod-product-compliance
Lightning Source LLC
Chambersburg PA
CBHW060110050426
42448CB00011B/2665